**Volu~**

# HOP Beginners Guide To Doing Safety Differently

# Human Error

*By Brent Sutton and foreword by Rob Fisher.*

© Learning Teams Inc 2024

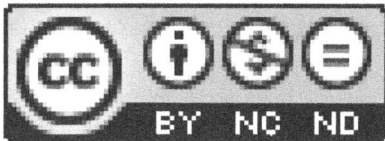
Published: May 2024
ISBN: 979-8883490728

# PROLOGUE

I am often asked, "Why do Jenga blocks appear in many HOP publications?".

The story is that the game Jenga Ⓡ[1] involves removing one block from a tower constructed of 54 blocks at a time. Each block removed is then placed on top of the tower, creating a progressively taller and unstable structure until someone's misstep (either on removing a block or on placing it unsteadily on top of the destabilizing structure) leads to it crashing down. This is the perfect analogy for the concepts of complexity in systems, as well as HOP (Human and Organizational Performance), which can be explored through several key perspectives:

■ **Fragility and Stability in Complex Systems:** A Jenga tower is a metaphor for complex systems, often composed of interconnected and interdependent elements. In Jenga, each block represents a component of the system. The tower's stability depends on each block's integrity and interaction. Similarly, removing or altering one element in complex systems can have unpredictable and potentially destabilizing effects on the entire system. This illustrates the fragile balance in complex organizations and ecosystems, where changes in one part can lead to significant and often unforeseen consequences in another.

---

[1] JENGA® is a registered trademark owned by Pokonobe Associates.

- **Incremental Change and Risk Management:** In Jenga, players take turns removing one block at a time, akin to making incremental changes in a system or organization. This process requires careful risk assessment and understanding each move's implications. It mirrors the decision-making process in organizations where people must evaluate the impact of their actions, balancing innovation and progress against the potential risks of destabilizing the system.

- **Adaptability and Learning:** As the game progresses, the structure becomes increasingly unstable, requiring players to adapt their strategies. This reflects the need for adaptability in complex systems and organizations. Organizations that can learn from their current environment and past events and adjust accordingly are more likely to succeed.

- **Interconnectedness and Team Dynamics:** Jenga is often played in teams, highlighting the importance of collaboration, communication, cooperation, and understanding the interconnectedness of work in a group setting.

- **Thresholds and Catastrophic Failure:** The collapse of a Jenga tower can be sudden and dramatic, illustrating the concept of thresholds in complex systems. Systems can absorb change up to a point, but a rapid and irreversible shift can lead to failure or collapse once a critical threshold is crossed. This concept is essential in understanding how systems can deteriorate or fail and the importance of recognizing and respecting limits in both natural and organizational environments.

- **Predictability and Uncertainty:** While the basic rules of Jenga are simple, predicting the outcome of each move becomes increasingly difficult as the game progresses. This unpredictability mirrors the inherent uncertainty in complex systems, where, despite having rules and controls, the exact outcomes of interactions within the system can be challenging to predict.

- **Feedback Loops:** The Jenga game demonstrates feedback loops, where each move affects the tower's stability and influences subsequent decisions. In complex systems, feedback loops play a crucial role, where the outcomes of actions can reinforce or undermine the system's stability.

The Jenga tower is a powerful metaphor for understanding the dynamics of complex systems, emphasizing the importance of balance, adaptability, risk assessment, and the interconnected nature of elements within a system. These concepts directly apply to the human performance of workers and the organization's performance, underscoring the need for awareness, adaptability, and learning of the broader impacts of system work design and conditions in complex environments.

HOP helps us make the system's complexity more visible or transparent and a way to support better work without too many "uh-oh, I messed up!" moments before the safety system collapses like a game of Jenga.

Brent Sutton

# Other books in this series

*Please note: This is subject to change.*

# FOREWORD

My name is Rob Fisher, and I am the President of Fisher Improvement Technologies. We have been teaching our clients how to do "safety differently" for over 30 years. When Brent told me he was writing the series A HOP Beginners Guide to Doing Safety Differently and asked me to write a few words, I immediately had a few thoughts.

First, I was honored to be asked to provide this foreword. Second, I couldn't think of a better person to help those in our community take their next logical step in improvement using the HOP principles.

You might think that the series should be written from the perspective of the history of HOP. I discovered through reading the books that, while history is important, it is more important to get the perspective from someone living it NOW and still paying homage to history. Brent has gone to great lengths to understand and describe the history where important, and still describe the what's and how's of the current state of deploying HOP successfully.

Many organizations have jumped on board "the HOP train" for varied reasons. The challenges are:

- They don't truly know what that means

- They don't understand. Just knowing the concepts doesn't get them where they want to go, and

- They either don't know the "hows" of deployment and integration of the concepts, OR they have only been exposed to one element of HOP, thinking that is all HOP is.

Using a creative mix of science, concepts, and stories (oh, the stories!), the series provides a process when followed, enables individuals and organizations to use the HOP concepts and create sustainable improvements. That is really what safety differently is all about.

As someone who has lived the HOP journey from its onset, I can surely say that Brent has wonderfully described and bundled A HOP Beginners Guide to Doing Safety Differently in a way that will help people successfully navigate their HOP journey.

Grab a cup of your favorite beverage, settle in someplace comfortable, grab your personal note-taking preference, and prepare to make the changes necessary for you and your organization to DO SAFETY DIFFERENTLY.

Remember, Intentional Leadership starts with YOU!

Rob Fisher
President, Fisher Improvement Technologies
Author: Understanding Mental Models ISBN: 979-8840842461

# INTRODUCTION

## WHY THE BOOK - BRENT SUTTON

In August 2023, I talked with Bobby Cowger about his HOP journey and what led him to his new podcast show, The HOPcast. I jokingly told Bobby that he was a HOP Millennial "HOPster," which I meant as a compliment. The conversation with Bobby made me think about how our workforce is changing, as the baby boomers and Gen X's make way for most of our workforce to Millennials and Gen Z. It made me think about how the HOP Principles and our emerging workforce align. I undertook some non-academic study into the topic and discovered that they;

- Want to have a say and contribute their ideas. They resist doing repetitive or tedious work. They desire to have a life outside of work and expect enough flexibility to allow them to fulfill both their personal and professional commitments.

- Want to be supported, receive feedback, be mentored, and feel appreciated. That doesn't make them dependent but quite strategic. They think about what they need to be successful, and that's what they ask for.

- Want work that enables them to contribute positively to society and appropriately rewards them. One isn't a substitute for the other.

- Are comfortable with technology but also believe that feeling like they have a community at work is a determining factor in organizational commitment, job satisfaction, engagement, and retention.

- Are committed when they mostly get what they need; they don't want to leave; they want to move up in the organization. But being committed isn't blind loyalty or staying no matter what.

I concluded that the HOP Principles and the values of our new workforce are closely aligned. And if more people like Bobby spread the word about HOP and if we baby boomers and Gen X support and mentor them on their journey of learning and improving, then there will be a learning and improving future for all of us.

This was the impetus for this book series. A series of beginner guides that explored HOP, tools, and integration themes for everyone (not just Millennials).

A book series written by non-academics for non-academics. A book series that was not only relatable to people but also created a call to action, "HOP Into Action®," which is our safety differently approach to building human capability, capacity, and resilience in all things HOP, using a scaffolded learning approach, which we call CCR®[2] (Capability, Capacity, and Resilience).

This book series has been designed to support this. We will help you to improve your;

- **Capability** of HOP knowledge and understanding through this body of knowledge and stories from real people.

- **Capacity** to go out into the real world and use the activities in the book to try out the concepts, themes, tools, and approaches to create the link between learning and improving.

---

[2] CCR (Capability, Capacity and Resilience) and HOP Into Action are trademarks for Learning Teams Inc.

■ **Resilience** as you learn, reflect, and adapt to the challenges you will encounter on your journey, using the learning, reflection, and coaching journal in each book.

We want you to start where you have experience so you can evaluate and assess the gap between where you are now and where you need to be. It is not about perfection; like all journeys, there will be bumps, and there need to be bumps. We learn from these bumps, and we improve from these bumps if we reflect.

Remember, look for the little wins; it is about winning the battle, not the war.

In closing, as a proud New Zealander, I leave you with these wise words from New Zealand explorer Sir Edmund Hillary, who was the first climber to reach the summit of Mt Everest in 1953.

It is not the mountain we conquer but ourselves.

You don't have to be a fantastic hero to do certain things -to compete.

You can be just an ordinary person, sufficiently motivated to reach challenging goals.

HOP principles are a desire to improve safety and reliability in organizations and a shift in thinking about how people behave and organizations function

# HOP PRINCIPLES RECAP

The five principles of HOP (in order of sense-making) are:

■ **Error Is Normal; People Make Mistakes**: This principle acknowledges that errors are a normal part of human behavior and should be expected. The focus should not be on the error itself but on creating systems that tolerate inevitable errors.

■ **Context Drives Behavior**: The conditions under which work is conducted greatly influence worker behavior. Good systems and processes help manage the uncertain operational outcomes that are always present in organizations.

■ **Blame Fixes Nothing**: Blaming individuals for mistakes does not improve operational efficiency. Instead, it discourages the disclosure of important operational data and hinders learning and improvement.

■ **How You Respond to Failure Matters**: Leaders can choose to use failures as opportunities for learning and improvement, or they can choose to punish those involved. The former approach encourages disclosure of information about failures and leads to organizational improvement, while the latter discourages such disclosure and hinders improvement.

■ **Learning and Improving is Vital**: Organizations have two choices when responding to failure: to learn and improve or to blame and punish. Choosing to learn from failures is a strategic choice toward improvement.

But try not to think of the HOP Principles as a list of commandments or an order in which they must be applied. The HOP Principles are more effective when working together as a mutual reliance (interdependent) instead of co-dependent on one another (meaning if one isn't present, the rest are ineffective).

We have used a "pictorial metaphor" of a pentagon to suggest the interdependent associations. For example, suppose a leader responds negatively to an event by blaming the actions of individuals. In that case, the ability for learning by the organization and the frontline workers will be reduced, and the broader system improvements may be limited by focusing on human error as the "cause and effect" of the event.

The HOP 5 Pentagon © Learning Teams Inc, 2024.

"To err is human, but to persist in error is only the act of a fool." - Marcus Tullius Cicero

This quote reflects the understanding that making mistakes is a natural part of being human, but learning from those mistakes and not repeating them is what truly matters. It emphasizes the importance of growth and learning from our errors rather than dwelling on them.

# CHAPTER ONE: WHAT IS HUMAN ERROR

## THE ORIGINS

We started making mistakes when we developed the mental process of "cognitive abilities" involved in knowing, learning, and understanding to make decisions and engage in behaviors. This capacity for error is a part of being human and is closely tied to our ability to learn, adapt, and evolve.

Making and learning from mistakes has been important for human development evolutionarily. Early humans who made errors in hunting for food or tool-making learned from these mistakes, which led to improved tool-making techniques and survival strategies. This process of trial and error has been fundamental in human evolution and continues to be a part of how individuals and communities grow and improve.

Yet framing "error" or "mistake" implies self-awareness and intention that would have developed alongside human consciousness.

As early humans evolved more complex brains, particularly the prefrontal cortex, which is involved in decision-making and social behavior, they would have become increasingly capable of actions that could be considered mistakes in hindsight.

So, while it's impossible to pinpoint an exact moment when humans started making mistakes, it's clear that the capacity for error has been a fundamental part of human experience throughout history and the future of all of us.

# THE LENS AND ROLE OF HINDSIGHT

It is natural to make a connection between errors and hindsight. In many cases, hindsight provides a clear perspective that was not available when a decision or action was made, leading to the recognition of errors. This phenomenon is often encapsulated in the saying, "Hindsight is 20/20."

There are good and bad sides to hindsight, and how we frame it matters. For example:

- **Recognition of Mistakes:** With hindsight, workers and the organization can recognize mistakes that were not apparent at the time. This is because hindsight allows for a more comprehensive evaluation of the safe system of work, the conditions in the work, and the situations that arose in normal work, including consequences and outcomes that were not foreseeable.

- **Decision-Making Process:** Hindsight can illuminate the decision-making process, revealing system flaws/brittleness or oversights. This can be particularly valuable in complex or high-stakes environments, where understanding the system causes of errors can lead to better decisions in the future.

- **Contextual and Situational Factors:** Hindsight often reveals the importance of contextual and situational factors that might have been overlooked or undervalued. This understanding can lead to a more nuanced approach to decision-making and problem-solving in similar contexts in the future.

- **Learning and Improvement:** Hindsight can be a powerful tool for learning and improvement. By understanding where and why errors occur, individuals and organizations can adapt and refine their strategies and actions to avoid similar mistakes in the future.

■ **Emotional and Psychological Impact:** Realizing errors through hindsight can have emotional and psychological impacts. It can lead to negative feelings of regret, guilt, or frustration, but it can also be a source of constructive reflection and personal growth.

---

It is natural for us to judge or blame in hindsight, and blame can feel good.

Yet, does blame allow us to learn and improve?

---

# THE ROLE OF BLAME

Blaming others can feel satisfying for several psychological reasons:

■ **Avoidance of Personal Responsibility:** Blaming others allows individuals to divert attention from their mistakes or shortcomings. By attributing faults or failures to external factors, individuals protect their self-esteem and avoid the discomfort of acknowledging their role in a negative outcome.

■ **Sense of Control and Understanding:** It can be unsettling and confusing when things go wrong. Blaming provides a simple explanation and gives a sense of understanding and control over the situation. It creates a narrative with a clear cause (the person being blamed), which can be psychologically comforting compared to the ambiguity of complex situations.

■ **Emotional Release:** Blaming can be an outlet for frustration, anger, and other negative emotions. It allows individuals to express their feelings and can provide a temporary sense of relief or catharsis.

■ **Simplification of Complex Situations:** The world is complex, and many situations involve multiple factors and nuances. Blaming simplifies this complexity by reducing the situation to a binary of right and wrong, with the blame placed firmly on someone else.

■ **Reinforcement of Group Cohesion:** In group settings, blaming an outsider or a specific member can strengthen the bonds within the rest of the group. It creates a sense of unity against a common 'enemy' or scapegoat.

■ **Cognitive Biases:** Cognitive biases like the fundamental attribution error (overestimating the role of personal characteristics in others' behavior while underestimating situational factors) and self-serving bias (attributing successes to individual factors and failures to external factors) contribute to the tendency to blame others.

Some of these were visible and emphasized during the COVID-19 pandemic, with our behaviors or behaviors of others that we didn't expect.

While blaming might offer temporary psychological relief or satisfaction, it is unproductive, can harm relationships, and hinder personal growth. It prevents learning from mistakes, fully understanding complex situations, and effectively resolving conflicts.

Recognizing the urge to blame as a psychological coping mechanism can help individuals approach situations more objectively and constructively.

# UNDERSTANDING HUMAN ERROR

Human error refers to the mistakes made by people rather than those caused by machines or systems. These errors can happen in any activity and are a natural part of being human. Here's a breakdown of the key points to understand human error:

## INEVITABILITY

No matter how skilled or careful we are, everyone makes mistakes. This is because humans aren't perfect, and our attention, memory, and judgment can be affected by various factors.

## COMMON FIXES OF HUMAN ERROR

While we can't eliminate human error, learning organizations can reduce error-likely situations in ways such as:

- **Designing Better Work:** Creating systems and processes that are understandable, useable, and can be applied in normal work, as well as safeguards to catch mistakes or reduce energy to the worker.

- **Knowledge Building and Situational Awareness:** Growing people's knowledge and skills, such as critical thinking and critical appraisal, assists us in better understanding how we function in work and when systems, conditions, or demands are changing.

- **Creating a Learning Environment**: Encouraging a learning culture where people can admit and learn from their mistakes rather than hiding them.

## UNDERSTAND ERROR IN THE CONTEXT OF WORK

Jens Rasmussen's framework on human performance modes is often applied in the HOP lens of work. He described how we perform tasks and make decisions in three main modes: skill-based, rule-based, and knowledge-based. Each mode reflects a different level of consciousness and decision-making, depending on the task or situation—the "error potential" baseline increases from skill-based to rule-based to knowledge-based.

| Performance Mode | Baseline Error Rate |
|---|---|
| Knowledge Mode | 1:2 to 1:10 |
| Rule Mode | 1:100 |
| Skill Mode | 1:1,000 |

## SKILL-BASED PERFORMANCE MODE

Think of this as auto-pilot or muscle memory. We do these tasks almost unconsciously because we've done them many times. Walking, typing on a keyboard, or even driving a familiar route can be skill-based. In high-risk industries, workers may train, apply, and reflect regularly to embed this learning. If errors in this mode happen, it is said that we are focused or thinking about something else, e.g., missing a turn while driving because we're deep in thought. Language like being distracted, not paying attention, or losing situational awareness are used to explain this when, in reality, we use skill-based performance to be highly successful in work. The following two pages are stories where Skill Mode was critical in determining a successful outcome and when a situation arose when Skill Mode created an unexpected outcome. Yet this error was only apparent in hindsight.

## Skill Mode for Success

Anna is an experienced bicycle courier. Her day is a constant challenge of tight deadlines, delivering packages to various clients across the city, and traffic flows. Anna's bicycle is an extension of herself; her movements are fluid and automatic after years of navigating the city. The city hosts a long weekend street festival during the summer. Street vendors and decorations partially obstruct the roads, and pedestrians are unpredictable. Anna's skill-based performance becomes her greatest asset. She anticipates the flow of the crowd, predicting movements before they happen, and her reflexes are sharp and attuned to the task.

Approaching a crowded intersection, a sudden movement catches her eye—a child breaks away from their parent, darting into the street to chase a stray balloon. Without hesitation, Anna's training kicks in. There's no time for conscious thought, only the action shaped by years of experience. She executes a maneuver, skirting the child with enough clearance to ensure their safety, her heart pounding but her hands steady. The child's parent, overcome with relief, calls out, "Thank you," as Anna nods, a small smile of acknowledgment on her face. She doesn't stop; the delivery clock is still ticking. As she pedals away, her mind barely registers the incident as out of the ordinary—it's all part of a day's work.

This demonstrates Anna's skill-based performance. There was no error, only the execution of expertise, a reminder of how deeply human capabilities can be ingrained through practice and repetition.

## Skill Mode for Unexpected Outcome

Marco is an experienced chef in a family restaurant. The dinner rush is at its peak, with orders from hungry families. Marco's hands work in a blur, effortlessly chopping, sautéing, and plating. Each movement is precise and honed from repetition, whereas skill-based performance is where thought and action merge. In preparation for the next order, Marco reached for a bottle of olive oil, his eyes and mind fixed on the next task. Without realizing it, he took a similar-shaped bottle of sesame oil. The mistake goes unnoticed as Marco drizzles the sesame oil over a pan of sizzling vegetables. It was a dish he had prepared a thousand times, a customer favorite that demanded no conscious thought, as it was part of simultaneous tasks demanding his attention.

The dish is taken to the customer's table. The error revealed itself in their first bites, the unexpected sesame flavor clashing with the garlic, tomato, and basil. The waiter observes confusion as the dinner guests inquire about the dish's unusual taste. Marco is frustrated by his mistake, which he believes only a rookie would make. He apologizes to the dinner guests and prepares a new dish.

The incident was a humbling reminder that even the most automatic, skill-based tasks are susceptible to error, especially where the ingredients look the same.

## RULE-BASED PERFORMANCE MODE

This is when we follow or need to apply instructions or rules that we've learned to complete tasks. It's like following a recipe or a manual. You use rule-based performance if you're cooking a new dish and following a recipe. Errors occur when we apply the wrong rule to a situation, like using a rule for baking a cake when you're trying to grill steak.

The following two pages are stories about how Rule-Based Mode was critical in determining a successful outcome and when a situation arose when Rule-Based Mode created an unexpected result. Yet this error was only apparent in hindsight.

## Rule-Based Mode for Success

Emma is a systems engineer in the control room of a power facility; her role and decision-making are mission-critical for supplying an essential service to a city. During a sweltering summer afternoon, the grid nears its capacity. Emma's eyes darted between screens, tracking consumption levels, transformer statuses, and potential fault lines. The rule book for grid management was etched into her mind, a catalog of protocols and procedures to ensure stability and safety.

Suddenly, an alarm blared. A grid segment showed rapidly escalating demand, threatening to overload and trigger a cascading blackout across the city. Emma's training kicked in immediately. She initiated the standard emergency load-shedding procedure—a series of deliberate power reductions to non-essential circuits to prevent the system from crashing.

As Emma directed her team in implementing the load shed sequence, her adherence to the rules ensured a smooth operation. Within minutes, the potential crisis was averted. The grid stabilized, and the risk of a blackout receded. The city remained unaware of the danger it had skirted. The lights stayed on, and the air conditioners continued to hum, providing much-needed relief from the summer heat.

The following debriefing recognized Emma's quick response and adherence to the rule-based procedures. Emma's ability to apply them without hesitation was a testament to her training and expertise. It is a reminder that, when faced with potential disaster, the clarity, doablility and understanding of the rules and procedures were the city's saving grace.

## Rule-Based Mode for Unexpected Outcome

Tom is an Air Traffic Controller. His role is critical. He orchestrates the ballet of incoming and outgoing flights with precision and care. The rules of air traffic control were his bible, guiding every decision to ensure safety and efficiency in the skies.

One foggy morning, as visibility dropped and the radar screens glowed more intensely with the signals of circling aircraft, Tom faced a challenging unfolding situation. A small private plane requests an emergency landing due to a critical fuel shortage. At the same time, a large commercial airliner is scheduled to land on the same runway, with the pilot following the standard flight schedule and airport protocols.

Tom relied on his skills and experience and the rule-based procedures that dictated the prioritization of commercial flights during peak hours. He instructed the private plane to continue circling, expecting that the situation could be managed within the aircraft's remaining fuel capacity. His decision is designed to maximize efficiency and minimize disruptions.

However, the private plane's fuel situation was more critical than Tom had assessed, and the minutes spent circling further depleted its reserves, bringing it dangerously close to a forced emergency landing outside the airport perimeter.

Continued on next page.......

The private plane pilot, realizing the gravity of the situation, issues a final, desperate plea with a Mayday call. Tom quickly adjusts his instructions, clearing the way for an immediate landing. The private plane lands safely, with mere moments to spare before running out of fuel.

The incident prompted a learning review of air traffic control protocols. Tom's reliance on the rigid application of rule-based performance highlighted the need for flexibility in emergencies and a reassessment of prioritization rules under unique circumstances.

This story was a learning opportunity for Tom and his colleagues, emphasizing the importance of balancing rule-based procedures with situational awareness and critical thinking. While the established rules provided a strong foundation for decision-making, this event was a stark reminder that exceptions could arise, demanding a departure from the rulebook in favor of immediate, situational judgment calls to ensure safety.

## KNOWLEDGE-BASED PERFORMANCE MODE

Knowledge-based performance mode kicks in when we face new situations or problems that we don't immediately know how to solve. We must think, analyze, and figure things out using knowledge and reasoning.

An example would be if you're trying to fix a leak in your plumbing for the first time without clear instructions. Errors in this mode can happen because we need more proper knowledge or because the problem is so complex that it's hard to solve on the first try.

The following two pages contain stories about how Knowledge-Based Mode created a successful outcome and when a situation arose when Knowledge-Based Mode created an unexpected result. Yet this error is only apparent in hindsight.

## Knowledge-Based Mode for Success

Marcus is an experienced construction manager overseeing the development of a new office building. The ambitious project incorporates eco-friendly materials and advanced technology to create a sustainable and energy-efficient structure. Halfway through the construction, Marcus encountered an unexpected challenge. The delivery of a critical, custom-made structural component was delayed due to manufacturing issues abroad, threatening to derail the project's timeline and significantly increase costs.

Marcus has faced many issues in the past that can impact project delivery and schedule. He is really good at thinking on his feet and problem-solving. Drawing upon his knowledge, he proposed an innovative solution. Instead of waiting for the delayed component, he suggested a temporary support structure constructed with locally available materials. This would allow work to continue on other building parts without compromising safety or overall structural integrity.

Marcus presented his plan to the project's engineers and architects, explaining the logic and science behind his approach. His solution was based on a deep understanding of load distribution and the properties of alternative materials that could temporarily bear the necessary weight. After a thorough analysis and some initial skepticism, the team agreed to implement Marcus's proposal.

Continued on next page.......

Construction continued, and Marcus's knowledge-based performance proved successful. When the original component finally arrived, the transition to the permanent structure was seamless.

The office building was completed on time, meeting all its ambitious environmental and technological goals. Marcus's leadership and knowledge-based performance saved the project from delay and reinforced his reputation as a forward-thinking and resourceful construction manager.

The project's success was a testament to the power of expertise and innovation in the face of unexpected challenges and to humans' ability to adapt and be resilient to challenging demands.

## Knowledge-Based Mode for Unexpected Outcome

An innovative architect, Rachel spearheads the construction of a pioneering mixed-use complex. Designed to be the epitome of modern living and sustainability, the project was Rachel's brainchild, blending cutting-edge architectural techniques with environmentally friendly materials.

Midway through the construction phase, Rachel faced a significant challenge. The project was set to incorporate a unique, transparent roofing material to improve natural lighting while maintaining energy efficiency. However, as the construction team began installing the roofing, Rachel realized the material's thermal properties were not performing as expected under the area's variable weather conditions. The building's interior became uncomfortably warm, casting doubt on the project's sustainability claims and potentially compromising its GREEN certification prospects.

Confronted with this, Rachel relied on her knowledge and experience to devise a solution. She proposed integrating an innovative but untested phase-changing material (PCM) into the roofing structure. Her idea was based on the knowledge that PCMs could absorb and release heat, stabilizing the building's internal temperature without additional energy consumption.

Continued on next page......

However, several weeks after the installation, it became evident that the PCM integration had not yielded the expected results. Instead of stabilizing temperatures, fluctuations in the building's internal environment became more pronounced, leading to discomfort for the workers and concerns from prospective tenants. The error in Rachel's knowledge-based performance stemmed from an overreliance on theoretical benefits without sufficient real-world testing in similar architectural applications.

This setback required a costly redesign of the roofing system and delayed the project's completion, affecting the budget and Rachel's reputation.

The project eventually achieved its sustainability goals, but Rachel's journey was a humbling experience.

# SO WHY DO WE MAKE ERRORS

Dr. James Reason was a psychology professor in the UK. His work, GEMS (Generic Error-Modelling System), takes Rasmussen's model more toward cognitive factors that lead to human error.

Cognitive factors are the human processes and mechanisms we use to acquire, process, store, and use information. This influences how we think, learn, remember, and make decisions at work and in life in areas such as;

■ **Attention**: How to focus on a task.

■ **Memory**: How we process, store, and retrieve information.

■ **Perception**: How we interpret information.

■ **Problem-Solving**: How we solve complex problems.

■ **Decision-Making**: How we choose different options or choices to act on.

■ **Language Processing**: How we understand and talk.

■ **Learning**: How we take on new knowledge and skills through experience or instruction.

Therefore, if we are all different as humans (meaning that we are not all the same), these factors play a crucial role in how we think, work, act, and make errors. Reason's GEMS model has four basic error types: slips and lapses (skill-based), rule-based and knowledge-based.

**Skill-Based Error (slips and lapses)**

Slips are actions that are different from what we intended to do (memory failures). For example, if you take a familiar route to work or home every day, you are on autopilot, and you take the correct exit without thinking about it, and your task is successful.

On the weekend, you take the family to an outdoor activity. The route uses the same familiar road, but two exits past where you usually turn off. The family is excited and talking about all the fun they are looking forward to as you drive to the destination. You turn off the exit and keep driving; a little voice from the back of the car can be heard: "Hey, Dad, why are we going to your work!".

This is a skill-based mistake. When you reached your work exit, you relied on your instinct and physically turned the steering wheel instead of consciously thinking about where you were going.

Ask yourself the question. In this situation, was the error an **action** (knowingly) or an **outcome** of familiarity?

> The same things that make you successful can also lead to error.

**Rule-Based Error:**

These mistakes involve judgment and decision-making.

You need to fill your work light truck with gas for the week, so you pump $60 because that's the "rule" you follow; that's what you always pump to last you for the work you do for the week.

However, gas prices go up, and you don't take into account that it now costs $80 to fill the tank. Now, you don't have enough gas for the week.

You made a rule-based mistake. This is not an action error (skill-based) because you did use some conscious decision-making, so it is referred to as a "thinking" error.

Ask yourself the question. In this situation, was the error an **action** (knowingly) or an **outcome** of familiarity?

The same things that make you successful can also lead to error.

**Knowledged-Based Error:**

This is a mistake that involves higher-level judgment and decision-making. You are driving back to the airport from a construction project in an unfamiliar city, but your route is now closed due to road repairs, and you are running late for the flight. Confident that you know the general direction to the airport, you decided to rely on his instincts and turn off the GPS, thinking it might only cause more confusion. As you drive through the city, you miss a crucial exit that leads directly to the highway connecting to the airport. You are now in a residential area with narrow streets and one-way lanes. Your initial confidence starts to wane as you try to return to the highway. You realize you have completely lost your way.

You made a knowledge-based error. You developed an immediate plan in response to the unexpected and unfamiliar situation because a decision was not reflexive, and you had no rules to follow, but it didn't work out.

Ask yourself the question. In this situation, was the error an **action** (knowingly) or an **outcome** of uncertainty?

> The same things that make you successful can also lead to error.

## PERFORMANCE MODE SUMMARY

Rasmussen's and Reason's models help us understand that human error exists in successful and unsuccessful work. When things go right, we may call them "Innovation and Adaptation," when they go wrong, we call them "Error, Deviation, and Violation."

Rasmussen's model helps us understand why we make mistakes based on how familiar we are with a task, whether following rules or trying to solve a new problem.

It shows that errors can happen in different ways and for various reasons, depending on how we think and act at the time and the system of work or conditions we operate in.

## WHY DO WE TREAT HUMAN ERROR AS A CURABLE ILLNESS

The problem of human error can be viewed in two ways: the person approach and the system approach.

Each has its model of error causation, and each model gives rise to different philosophies of error management. Understanding these differences has important practical implications for coping with the risk.

**It is a people problem:** The long-standing and widespread tradition of the person approach focuses on the unsafe acts—errors and procedural violations—of people on the front line. It views these unsafe acts as arising primarily from aberrant mental processes such as forgetfulness, inattention, poor motivation, carelessness, negligence, and recklessness. The associated countermeasures are directed mainly at reducing unwanted variability in human behavior. These methods include poster campaigns that appeal to people's fear, writing another procedure (or adding to existing ones), disciplinary measures, threat of litigation, retraining, naming, blaming, and shaming. Followers of these approaches tend to treat errors as moral issues, assuming that bad things happen to bad people—what psychologists have called the "just-world hypothesis" in the belief that the world is fair and, consequently, that the moral standings of our actions will determine our outcomes.

> This viewpoint causes us to believe that those who do good will be rewarded, and those who exhibit negative behaviors will be punished and need a dose of their own medicine, believing that human error is an illness that can be cured.

**It is a system problem:** The basic premise in the system approach is that humans are fallible and errors are to be expected, even in the best organizations. Errors are seen as consequences rather than causes, having their origins not so much in the perversity of human nature as in "upstream" systemic factors. These include recurrent error traps in the workplace and the organizational processes that give rise to them. Countermeasures are based on the assumption that although we cannot change the human condition, we can change the conditions under which humans work. The central idea is that of system defenses. All hazardous technologies possess barriers and safeguards. When an adverse event occurs, the important issue is not who blundered but how and why the defenses failed.

This people versus system problem is also visible in our safety management system with policies and procedures. A leading academic in this space of Safety Science, Professor Erik Hollnagel said:

> Safety can be a condition where the number of unacceptable outcomes are as low as possible, or
>
> Safety is a condition where the number of acceptable outcomes is as high as possible.

This is the difference between "**Managing Safety**" versus "**Managing Safely**".

The HOP lens supports this notion of "Managing Safely" with the HOP Principles and language such as;

---

People can fail but fail safely.

The system can fail but fail gracefully.

Workers are only as safe as they need to be.

---

How people perform in the system is essential, and removing "error-likely situations" by understanding performance modes helps us build better work, and learning from why works goes right is valuable than waiting to learn by work goes wrong.

We must have controls, barriers, and defenses (safeguards) in place for the inevitability of human error when work involves energy that can harm or kill us (STKY - S**t That Can Kill You).

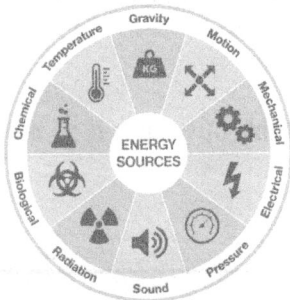

---

Design and build better, more error-tolerant systems because systems and context drive behavior, and people will make mistakes.

---

# THE ROLE OF ACCOUNTABILITY AND RESPONSIBILITY

When things go wrong (Events, Accidents, and Incidents), the opportunity for learning can be diminished or squandered by those in leadership or management roles because of their beliefs around accountability and responsibility. When organizations investigate incidents and accidents, they interview, gather facts, analyze that information, determine causes and failings, and generate corrective actions that typically add more layers of controls, mitigations, barriers, and rules than before.

The investigation becomes a retributive intervention by asking questions like:

- Which rule has been broken?
- What happened? Who did it?
- How bad was it?
- Do you realize there will be consequences if you take risks?
- And that there will be even more consequences if you are negligent.

And the investigation report will be a **Name**, **Blame**, **Shame**, **Re-train** and **Write a new procedure**.

**Here is how it works:**

Leaders aim to reduce injury rates or zero harm because that is how safety progress is measured. If someone gets injured, the organization finds someone to blame. That individual is shamed, typically publicly or in a report, safety alert, company stand-down, etc, for causing the event. Then, everyone is trained not to do what that individual did, and we write a new rule or procedure to "dumb down" what the organization wants workers to do.

Few leaders will admit that this is an intentional safety strategy. Who would want to? It sounds like a terrible strategy. But when you look at many actual practices, that is what they do.

Here are some signs of that in your system;

- **Incentives for target incident rates**. If an individual or a team doesn't hit the target rate, they don't earn the reward.

- **Focus on accident investigation and root cause analysis**. You must find THE root cause, and often, it's a person.

- The most frequent corrective action is training or other administrative controls about correcting people to the expected rules or behaviors.

- The walls of your workplace are covered with posters urging people to "**work safe**" and "**safety first**."

- And you run **Safety Campaigns** reminding people what not to do.

Yet, let us not blame leaders; that only perpetuates the circle of blame. Understand that leaders have committed and invested significant time, money, and resources in creating safety systems, procedures, safe work practices, and life-saving rules; there is a belief that there is no way the system failed; it had to be human error.

When leaders hear about an accident, they immediately respond, "I know exactly what happened." That is how investigations are influenced (often subconsciously) to achieve the outcome company leaders anticipated. We know it doesn't make the workplace or the work safer because we aren't eliminating or reducing the energy of the hazard. Tragically, in the short term, this strategy works because we see an initial drop in the number of accidents but then reach a plateau they can't seem to break through.

> This is a retributive approach to safety; you can't punish your way to compliance.

You can't punish your way to compliance.

## RETRIBUTION IMPLIES GUILT

People believe that retribution may come from a place where we are trying to make things fairer and more accountable at the same time. The issue with retribution is:

- ▪ ·Who draws those lines?

- ▪ Who gets to decide what behavior is coupled with what?

- ▪ Who gets to decide what risky conduct is?

- ▪ Who gets to decide what negligence is?

- ▪ Can you determine if an unsafe act or action was made unconsciously versus consciously?

The line is never clear when you are a judge, jury, and executioner.

This position is justified with words like accountability, responsibility, culpability, and conduct. They mean the same thing. They all mean discipline in some form or another.

---

**Accountability is a willingness to accept responsibility or to account for one's actions.**

---

Accountability isn't punishment; it's not retribution or culpability. It's not something you can do to a person, demand from them, dictate or extract from them, or punish people into compliance with.

So, when I think about what real accountability looks like in practice, I think about Learning Teams. In essence, with a Learning Team, a group of workers constructs a framework for trust, openness, transparency, and accountability by:

- **Recognizing** the role of the worker and their contribution to that work on the day of the event (being responsible)

- **Understanding** how work on the day of the event happened, compared to normal everyday work (being accountable)

- **Showing** how work, systems, or tools could be improved (being responsible)

- Be able to work together on **developing** the **learnings** and **improvements** from that event to improve the "safety of work" and "work operations" to reduce occurrence in the future (being accountable and responsible for all)

# THE HOP LENS OF ACCOUNTABILITY AND RESPONSIBILITY

Human and Organizational Performance understands that the roles of accountability, responsibility, and culpability in the context of human performance and safety are nuanced and distinct, emphasizing a shift from blame to learning and improvement.

## ACCOUNTABILITY

Accountability is implicitly addressed through the principles that discourage the practice of blaming individuals for errors and instead encourage understanding the systemic factors that contribute to mistakes. Accountability should be oriented towards creating an environment where errors are seen as opportunities for learning and improvement rather than occasions for punishment.

The principles"Blame Fixes Nothing" and " How Leaders Respond to Failure Matters" highlight the importance of leaders creating a culture where accountability is about being answerable for ensuring systems are improved.

Learning is applied rather than merely being responsible for outcomes.

# RESPONSIBILITY

Responsibility in this context is mainly about the role individuals and organizations play in fostering a culture of safety and continuous improvement.

It involves proactively identifying potential errors and system weaknesses before incidents occur. The emphasis on learning and improving underscores the responsibility of both leaders and workers to engage in practices that enhance safety and reliability, such as understanding the context of errors and focusing on system improvements rather than individual blame.

---

HOP promotes a culture of accountability and responsibility centered around learning, improvement, and systemic change rather than individual blame and culpability.

This approach aims to enhance the safety and reliability of work environments by focusing on the underlying system causes of errors and incidents rather than the symptoms, behaviors, and outcomes, which are obvious in hindsight.

---

# CHAPTER TWO: HOP IN PRACTICE

## WAYS TO APPLY THE PRINCIPLES

Applying the 5 Principles of HOP in practice involves a shift in thinking and approach to safety and reliability in the workplace. Here's how you can apply each principle:

1. **Error is normal. Even the best people make mistakes.** Recognize that errors are a part of human nature and build systems that anticipate and mitigate these errors so that "people can fail safely" or "the system can fail gracefully" in managing the presence or transfer of energy from the event that could cause harm.

2. **Blame fixes nothing.** Instead of blaming individuals for errors, focus on understanding why the error occurred and how the system allowed it. This involves fostering a culture of open communication and learning, where employees feel safe to report errors and near misses.

3. **Learning and Improving is vital. Learning is deliberate.** Encourage continuous learning and improvement. This could involve regular training sessions, learning from everyday work in the field, near misses and incidents, and constantly seeking ways to improve safety protocols and work design.

4. **Context influences behavior. Systems drive outcomes.** Understand that the work environment and systems in place heavily influence employee behavior. Regularly review and improve these systems to ensure they promote and allow safe behavior.

5. **How you respond to failure matters. How leaders act and respond counts.** Leaders should respond to failures in a way that promotes learning and improvement, rather than blame. This could involve conducting thorough incident investigations to understand how the failure occurred and how to prevent it in the future rather than punishing individuals for errors. Moving from "**who failed**" (the person) to "**what failed**" (the system).

Remember, these principles should guide the development, implementation, and improvement of your safety systems, procedures, worker engagement, and the overall safety culture of the organization.

They should be communicated and discussed to all workers and ingrained in the organization's culture as **"how we do things around here"** commitment and ownership by leadership.

# HOP ACTIVITY

## INTRODUCTION

In this activity, we are looking for the presence of two HOP principles;

■ The system drives context and behavior

■ Error is normal, people make mistakes

And for you to reflect on those engagements and conversations with people. This is also an excellent opportunity to have a leader or colleague you work with or someone you see as a coach or mentor "**learning buddy**". Your role is to undertake the activity and then reflect. The other person's role is to listen, reflect, and provide observations on the HOP principles.

The five principles of HOP are:

Learning is vital for improvement

Error is normal, people make mistakes

Leaders response matters

System drives context and behavior

LEARNING

ERROR

LEADERS

SYSTEM

HOP 5

BLAME

Blame fixes nothing

The HOP 5 Pentagon © Learning Teams Inc, 2024.

## THINKING ABOUT YOUR JOURNEY OF LEARNING

During the exercise, there will be places to write. Think of this as a way to reflect on your learning journey. Your writing should not be a purely descriptive account of what you did and learned. It is an opportunity to communicate your thinking process about:

■ How and why, you did what you did?

■ What you now think about what you did?

■ What you can do differently next time?

When we reflect, we are more likely to develop a deeper understanding of ourselves, how we learn, and what we need to do to gain further skills. When we apply reflective practice, we are:

■ More motivated as we know what we are trying to achieve and why.

■ Use our existing knowledge to help us to develop our understanding of new ideas.

■ Understand new concepts by relating them to our previous experiences.

■ Develop our learning and thinking by building on the critical evaluation of our prior learning experiences.

■ More self-aware and able to identify, explain, and address their strengths and weaknesses.

---

> "Self-reflection is a humbling process. It's essential to find out why you think, say, and do certain things – then better yourself." – Sonya Teclai"

---

## APPLYING PRACTICE

Think of a job, task, or activity that people do in your organization that has a hazard that could cause life-changing or life-altering harm. Ideally, two or more people perform this job, task, or activity, and the hazard has a life-saving, critical, or cardinal rule linked to it. In many organizations, these rules remind workers of the measures they should or shouldn't take to protect their own safety. They draw attention to the activities most likely to lead to a fatality and the life-saving actions an individual controls. Examples of such rules are:

- Exclusion zones (e.g., when lifting operations occur or to separate workers from mobile plant and equipment)

- Energy Isolation (e.g., the use of lock out - tag out procedures)

- Working At Height (e.g., blanket height limit or use of fall arrest system)

- Do not exceed speed limits

- Keep clear of danger zones on machinery (e.g., nip points, crush zones)

Ask that small group of people (2 to 5) that you want to learn more about what they do by asking questions and listening to their stories about everyday work. Make sure they know that you are doing this as a learning exercise, and feel free to share with them about HOP and the five principles; it will help to make them curious. Remember, this is more than asking as many questions as possible or trying to learn about everything they do. The group will respond to you once they see that they are being listened to, respected, able to share stories, encouraged to participate, and recognized as experts in their work. And please remember;

---

"The greatest enemy to learning is knowing." – John C. Maxwell

---

## PART ONE: LEARNING QUESTIONS FROM THE WORKGROUP

Write down the job, task, or activity you are learning about.

|  |
|---|
|  |
|  |
|  |

Write down the "life-saving or cardinal rule" that workers must rely on.

|  |
|---|
|  |
|  |
|  |
|  |
|  |
|  |
|  |
|  |
|  |
|  |
|  |
|  |
|  |
|  |
|  |

**Question:** When doing that work, what is the hazard (STKY - Stuff That Can Kill You)?

**Question:** What do you rely on to stay safe?

**Question:** When applying the "life-saving rule" to do your work safely, do you have to?

| Rule Option | Yes or No |
|---|---|
| Change the work to comply with the rule | |
| Change the rules to get the work done | |
| Make new rules to get the work done | |
| Not use the rules to get the work done | |

**Question:** When applying the "life-saving rule" to do your work safely, has the rule worked in every scenario so far?

|  |
|---|
|  |
|  |
|  |

**Question:** How accessible, doable, and relatable are your procedures?

|  |
|---|
|  |
|  |
|  |
|  |
|  |
|  |
|  |
|  |
|  |
|  |

**Question:** What do you do to make the job easier?

**Question:** Can you share a story when something didn't go as planned, and you believe it could have gone wrong or did go wrong?

## PART TWO: YOUR REFLECTION

Write down your learnings and reflections on the stories shared by the group against the HOP principles.

**Write:** Your thoughts about how error is normal and how even the best people can make mistakes.

| |
|---|
| |
| |
| |
| |
| |
| |
| |
| |

**Write:** Your thoughts about whether the system and rules are designed to support "good and successful" work.

| |
|---|
| |
| |
| |
| |
| |
| |
| |
| |

**Write:** What are your thoughts about how the context of workers sharing their stories was evidenced in their behavior with you?

**Write:** What are your thoughts about how the organization sees successful work compared to the workers who do the work and face the risk every day?

## PART THREE: SHARING AND FEEDBACK WITH OTHERS

Take the opportunity to share your Part One: Learning Questions and
Part Two: Reflections with your learning buddy.

**Question:** What did you learn from this activity?

_____

**Question:** What did your learning buddy take from this activity?

_____

**Question:** Discuss and record with your learning buddy how you could take these learnings and apply them in a small way in your work each day.

**Question:** Discuss and record with your learning buddy what other opportunities you could find to share your learnings with others.

## ADDITIONAL RESOURCES

You can download PDF versions of Parts One, Two, and Three at:

https://hoptool.com/46ZTZcV or scan the QR code below.

You can access some free videos about Human Error courtesy of Rob Fisher, Fisher Improvement Technologies at:

https://hoptool.com/4a2v7Sx or scan the QR code below.

This is the beginning of your journey, and you can't go out and fix everything. Creating sustainable change happens in small increments.

# CHAPTER THREE: REFLECT ON YOUR LEARNINGS

## MY THOUGHTS MOVING FORWARD – BRENT SUTTON

Attributing workplace events to human error and blame provides simplicity and emotional satisfaction compared to the more complex and productive approach to understanding systemic issues.

Being able to make mistakes is an inherent aspect of human performance; therefore, errors are not only normal but expected. Focusing on human error as the primary cause of events is a simplistic approach that overlooks the underlying systemic vulnerabilities that allow these errors to lead to significant consequences.

Leaders often use blame as an emotionally satisfying response because it provides a clear target for our frustrations and a sense of justice being served. However, this approach is operationally ineffective as it misdirects attention and resources away from identifying and addressing the systemic causes. Blame creates an environment of fear and concealment, where individuals are less likely to report mistakes or near-misses, thereby depriving the organization of valuable learning opportunities.

The organizational and operational environment significantly influences individual and workgroup actions "context drives behavior". HOP challenges the notion of safety as solely a matter of personal responsibility and highlights the importance of designing work systems that support safe and successful everyday work.

By focusing on the context in which individuals operate, organizations can identify and mitigate systemic issues that predispose them to errors rather than merely reacting to mistakes after they occur.

This approach recognizes human error as a symptom of broader organizational and operational deficiencies. By focusing on understanding and addressing these systemic issues, organizations can build a culture of safety that is proactive, resilient, and conducive to continuous learning and improvement. This not only enhances safety but also contributes to the overall operational excellence of the organization.

> The HOP principles not only enhance safety but also contribute to the overall operational excellence of the organization.

# THE AUTHORS

**Brent Sutton**

Brent is well regarded as a safety coach and for taking organizations on a learning journey to understand how people are seen as the solution, how to engage people and leverage their skills so that worker participation becomes a normal way of running an organization where everybody benefits. Brent is the co-author of the best selling books on Learning Teams, Learning From Everyday Work, The 4Ds for HOP and Learning Teams, and host of the podcast show "The Practice of Learning Teams" and "HOP Into Action". He resides in Auckland, New Zealand.

**Rob Fisher**

Rob spent almost ten years in the US Navy before working at the South Texas Nuclear Project for twelve years, and has been involved in the evolution of HOP from its early days of HP and HPI.

Rob is the President and Director of Operations of Fisher Improvement Technologies. He has consulted for over one hundred companies in various fields including manufacturing, petrochemical, power generation (nuclear and non-nuclear), power transmission and distribution, and numerous Department of Energy sites. Rob is the author of the book Understanding Mental Models ISBN: 979-8840842461.

Made in the USA
Monee, IL
08 August 2024